INVEST IN THE NOW

JORDAN KIMMEL

© Copyright 2022 - All rights reserved.

The content contained within this book may not be reproduced, duplicated or transmitted without direct written permission from the author or the publisher.

Under no circumstances will any blame or legal responsibility be held against the publisher, or author, for any damages, reparation, or monetary loss due to the information contained within this book, either directly or indirectly.

Legal Notice:
This book is copyright protected. It is only for personal use. You cannot amend, distribute, sell, use, quote or paraphrase any part, or the content within this book, without the consent of the author or publisher.

Disclaimer Notice:
Please note the information contained within this document is for educational and entertainment purposes only. All effort has been executed to present accurate, up to date, reliable, complete information. No warranties of any kind are declared or implied. Readers acknowledge that the author is not engaged in the rendering of legal, financial, medical or professional advice. The content within this book has been derived from various sources. Please consult a licensed professional before attempting any techniques outlined in this book.

By reading this document, the reader agrees that under no circumstances is the author responsible for any losses, direct or indirect, that are incurred as a result of the use of the information contained within this document, including, but not limited to, errors, omissions, or inaccuracies.

Contents

Foreword by Jeffrey Hirsch i

Introduction 1

Chapter One 11
Your Mindset Can Be A Superpower

Chapter Two 23
Be Your Own Magnet

Chapter Three 35
Living A Happy Life

Chapter Four 45
Present Moment Living

Chapter Five 55
Meditation

Chapter Six 65
Being Mindful in your Personal and Professional Life by Ritika Hiranandani

Chapter Seven 75
Start Investing NOW

Significance of the Number 108 83

Epilogue 86

FOREWORD

■

Jeffrey Hirsch
Editor-in-Chief at Stock Trader's Almanac

Back in the late 1990s my late father Yale Hirsch, founder and creator of the *Stock Trader's Almanac*, was one of those Wall Street icons Jordan talks about seeking out and meeting. Yale was a welcoming man and welcomed the opportunity to meet Jordan. Jordan came to our office not long after I had joined the firm full time. It has been a dynamic, collegial friendship over the past 25 years or so, exchanging ideas, debating analyses, and most importantly learning from each other at every turn.

Quotations have inspired me my entire life. Since the first days of the *Almanac*, we have included motivating quotes that span the wit and wisdom of the ages in the *Almanac* on every day of the year on the weekly planner pages. As a child, I grew up observing my father seek out, highlight, collect and publish these meaningful and entertaining maxims. From antiquity to the present, he discovered them in books, plays, interviews, newspapers, and stock market outlooks. They came from famous playwrights, historical figures, eminent fund managers, and little-known market technicians. My high school senior yearbook page was mostly a collection of quotations, admittedly a little more rock and roll than the *Almanac*.

When I took over the business and the *Almanac* at the outset of the 21st century it become my responsibility and privilege to personally maintain and curate our database of quotations. I still take great pride and joy in uncovering new and old quotes alike from the words of billionaire investors to ancient polymaths to modern fintech influencers.

In fact, it was one of Jordan's dreams to be quoted in the *Almanac* – a dream that came true. As you read this book and begin to comprehend the wealth of wisdom, knowledge, and inspiration Jordan has accumulated you will come to understand how easy it was for his words to make the Almanac quotation cut. These are two Jordan quotes from my database:

Establish a no excuse environment – you will find your own quality will increase as well.

Discipline always makes hard work easy.

So, when Jordan tapped me for this project to review his book of quotations and write the forward it was a no brainer. I was flattered and honored and jumped at the chance.

Then when I finally received and read the manuscript

from Jordan and his team I was blown away. It was uplifting and inspiring and focused on the importance of a positive mindset. Make no mistake this is still an investment book, an investment book that inspires the reader to put aside the plethora of information we are all bombarded with nowadays, simplify and *Invest in the Now*!

Jordan and I both have a long-term time horizon when it comes to investing and wealth management, but we are both always focused on the present. What is driving the market today. What is working now. Where are the best values and opportunities in stocks, sectors, and asset classes. *Invest in the Now* short and sweet. It is refreshingly to the point – concise, succinct, salient. The book encapsulates my most favorite quote: *Brevity is the soul of wit.* — William Shakespeare.

Invest in the Now is a consolidation and amalgamation of everything Jordan has learned in 40 years on The Street. All the books he's read, the trades he's made, the clients he has helped, the personal and professional growth he has acquired. When I finished the book my first thought was, this book is like the Cliff Notes of Napoleon Hill's *Think and Grow Rich*! In today's TLDR world of 280 characters, sound bites and memes, Jordan gets right to the point in this energizing treatise on how to invest and how to get started, now. I know you will enjoy this fast read and come away ready to *Invest in the Now*. So don't delay, get started!

I will leave you a few favorite apropos quotes:

"Life is an illusion. You are what you think you are."
— Yale Hirsch
(Creator of Stock Trader's Almanac, 1923-2021)

"To change one's life: Start immediately. Do it flamboyantly. No exceptions."
— William James
(Philosopher, psychologist, 1842-1910)

"Make each day your masterpiece."
— John Wooden
(Coach, 1910-2010)

"The man who can master his time can master nearly anything."
— Winston Churchill
(British statesman, 1874-1965)

INTRODUCTION
∎

I'm Jordan Kimmel, author, investor, and I am a firm believer in the here and now. I've discovered the power of investing in the NOW for myself, and it's changed my life. I'm here to share how my life changed for the better when I started paying attention to the NOW. It worked for me, and I believe it can work for you too.

This book is, by design, a short book that can direct you into a way of stepping into the happiness that each of us deserves. Being in the NOW is key to unlocking the joy that is available in every moment.

The underlying theme running throughout the book is unconditional acceptance of "what is NOW". Take this opportunity to join us on this journey. If you can change your mindset, you can change your world. Getting yourself in the NOW is the missing piece in the noisy world around us.

What do you have to be willing to give up to be in the NOW? Basically nothing! All of your thoughts and words from the past serve as a kind of software that inhibits you from seeing or feeling anything new.

The past does not repeat itself, but it rhymes.

MARK TWAIN

The future rhymes because we keep repeating the same patterns from the past. We use the conditioning that was ingrained in us from past events and it continues into future events.

Ever wonder why you keep attracting the same kind of people into your life? Or you find yourself dealing with the same problems weeks, months, or even years later. There's a reason for that.

It's the patterns from the past that seep into the present. If you don't address these patterns, you'll find yourself in a bad remake of the classic 1993 movie '*Groundhog Day*'.

Dwelling on the past and much of what often clutters your mind keeps the past alive and prevents you from personal growth. We know a picture can tell 1000 words. A quote can often crystalize a life lesson and introduce or summarize an entire way of thinking.

The 108 quotes contained within this book can provide the key to unlocking your mind and placing you into the NOW while opening you to a new level of joy. Some of these quotes come from us personally while others come from some of the world's most recognized leaders and celebrities. Why are there 108 quotes? Continue reading this book to find out…

▎LIVING IN THE NOW

Living in and fully experiencing the NOW is a personal choice for me, and for very personal reasons. I grew up in a family with a very strong mother who worked with my father while owning and running a small retail women's boutique in New York City. With four children in the family, money was always tight, although as the youngest, I did not even realize it.

By the time I was of college age, my parents' business had grown, and they were fortunate enough to experience a significant financial windfall with an individual stock that provided them an opportunity to improve their lifestyle. Despite their improved financial position, I was told if college was in my future, I would be paying my own way. My parents simply explained that they had sacrificed for years while providing a comfortable lifestyle for their four children and were going to enjoy themselves at this time in their lives.

Only a few years later, my mother was taken shockingly early from this world by an aggressive cancer that rocked our family. A few years later, my father was also taken too soon, also from cancer. No longer did the expectations of working and saving until retirement age and then living in the "golden years" to 100 mean anything to me. Looking back, I am glad my parents enjoyed some special vacations together and even took some extravagant cruises while I was paying my way through college. Seeing my parents taken from the world at such young ages had a profound effect on me. I realized then the importance of living in the NOW and not taking the future for granted. Plan for the future, but living in the NOW became my way of being.

I was fortunate to attend one of the top high schools in the country, The Bronx High School of Science. There I was exposed to some great teachers and concepts. Something that I came to understand early through my studies was the concept of the bell curve. It is a simple concept but had a profound effort on the way I think. Whenever you have enough data points within a sample and use statistical analysis, things tend to fall under a "bell curve".

That is true with the height of buildings and humans, the IQ of humans, and almost anything that can be measured and ranked. Having seen my parents and grandparents achieve financial rewards in the stock market, I endeavored to create a model that would rank public companies and then set out to invest in only those companies that fell into the "right tip of the bell curve".

For those interested in the backstory and math, I outlined this extensively in my prior books, *Magnet Investing* and *The Magnet Method of Investing*. I am proud of the contributors in the books and the endorsements of those books by many of the top professionals in the world of finance. In this book, I simply want to emphasize the importance of being, living, and investing in the NOW.

As life unfolded, paying for my own college and attending a state college, a funny thing happened. It turned out that my college of choice, Stony Brook University, had several math professors who directed much of their attention to a relatively new field of quantitative financial analysis. New computer technology became available to analyze companies that simply did not exist previously.

In what now seems miraculous to me, the co-founder of my graduate program at Stony Brook University subsequently became my director of research at my own company, The Magnet Investment Group. There, he helped me create the first true blend of three unique investment approaches: value, growth, and momentum. Dr. T. Owen Carroll said at the time it was simply serendipity.

> *Learning from the past is critical, worrying about the future is pointless, my goal is to understand and invest in what is happening NOW.*
>
> **JORDAN KIMMEL**

▮ THE MAGNET® STOCK SELECTION PROCESS

The Magnet® Stock Selection Process operates in the NOW. Magnet ranks companies according to what is going on NOW, not what we hope or expect to happen in the future. Developed by a team including quantitative Ph. Ds, data scientists, and myself, Magnet ranks public companies based on several fundamental factors of financial strength, stability, and growth.

Simple clear and measurable factors, including current revenue growth, profit margins, and cash flow, are measured for all companies. This unbiased process simply but powerfully allows us to determine what is happening NOW. As a money manager, I am aware that my most important asset is not the biggest current position in my portfolio. I do not hold onto beliefs or positions simply because, in the past, those securities ranked highly on our Magnet® Model and helped create wealth. Things change, and it is always my focus to ask what is going on in the present. Therefore, I consider my biggest asset to be my mindset —to be in the present moment and hold a portfolio of companies that rank highest in the Magnet® Model NOW.

Many investment professionals and journals focus on trying to predict the future and then plan on how to position a portfolio based upon those assumptions. The more experience you have, the more you realize how off base most of the predictions end up being and how poorly the results turn out to be. This is not because most investment professionals are dumb or ill-intended, but because the world is so unpredictable and uncertain.

Magnet® Stocks attract other investors because of the revenue growth, profit margin growth, and increasing market share within their industry. The attraction to these growth traits is as natural as nature. I do not invest in the stock market; I invest in the current Magnet® Stocks—the ones that rank up the highest on our model—NOW.

I am guessing that as you are reading this, you already have your own way of identifying "superlatives"—or things that are currently better than worse based on your own expertise. Perhaps you have a certain advantage based upon your profession, knowledge base, or even your perception.

The key is to use your experience of being in the now to be able to identify current winners. Many years ago, one of the greatest mutual fund managers, Peter Lynch of the Fidelity Magellan fund, credited his wife by recognizing Hugs as something that was being worn by women at the time. It was a new product that was taking the country by storm, and he invested in the company that was making Hugs.

Lynch promoted the concept of "being aware" and investing in what you know. More recently, it could have been discovering Lululemon or Ulta Beauty as current Magnets — without using any math or elaborate formulas! Sports are bigger than ever, but usually not a single player from one decade to another is in the major league baseball All-Star game that is played annually.

Love stories are enjoyed over the years, but the actors change over time. It is very similar to the stock market.

In one of my previous books, *The Magnet Method of Investing*, I shared the theory of the "S curve". It is well known in the field of biology. Living organisms experience periods of growth followed by eventual decay. This is the simple life cycle—and it holds true with baseball players, actors, Sequoia trees, and public companies. I am keenly aware that fortunes were lost with a focus on the past. Many former stock market darlings created misery for investors that were anchored to a former reality that had passed.

Ask those who could not stay in the present moment and instead hung on to former glory. This list includes RCA, Eastman Kodak, Bethlehem Steel, Pan AM, AOL, Blockbuster Video, and General Electric. These are just some great high-profile examples to learn from. It is my intention to own a portfolio of the currently highest-rated Magnet® Stocks—NOW!

Change is inevitable and unstoppable. The competition in business and for business allows for new nimble companies to overtake the older and slower-moving companies that once dominated their industry. But the expression "the more things change, the more they remain the same" holds true in this case. The companies that currently have the best fundamentals NOW become the new Magnet® Stocks that our model uncovers and invests in. Whether investing in the stock market or living life to the fullest, focusing on the NOW and not the past is the key to success, happiness, and health.

Overall, whether in life or in investing, being at ease and focused in the NOW is the key. Do not be concerned about what will change. Any investment manager who tells you they know what will happen in the future is kidding you and themselves. Being in the present moment and focusing on what is happening now will allow you to tune out the noise from the phony fortune tellers, and not be haunted by the past.

It may turn out that you once made an investment in a particular business that did not work out. Maybe the time was not right back then, but it is NOW. Although I have shared my investing approach here, this is not only an "investment book". It is a book about having the right mindset to invest and enjoy your life.

This book has been a work in progress for almost a decade. Back then, I first met Trisha Bollman. Trisha talked about being in the present moment and not being caught up in the past. We talked about how similar her beliefs and my Magnet® Model were. By focusing on what was going on NOW, the future would take care of itself. At about the same time, I also met Ritika Hiranandani. Ritika was a business consultant at a financial firm that I was associated with. She spoke about the clarity that her meditation and yoga practice brought out in her. Funny, but Trisha had made a similar comment. We thought about creating a book that was able to share the idea of having the proper mindset that allows people to live better, invest better, and get the most out of life. Once we experienced a global lockdown and realized how much this book was needed, it all just unfolded. We knew how we each loved to collect quotes, and the book seemed to just come together. Despite the busy careers of Trisha and Ritika, I asked them to help write and finalize the book. We hope you find it helpful and inspiring and enjoy it as much as we loved creating it.

HOW TO INVEST IN THE NOW

Tip #1

Become empowered by realizing that nobody really knows what the future holds.

Tip #2

Understand what is going on NOW and invest in current Magnet® Stocks.

Tip #3

Understand that today's Magnet® Stocks will not be attracting other investors forever.

Tip #4

Be accepting that when a Magnet stock loses its attraction you will be able to simply move on to the next Magnet® Stocks that emerges.

Chapter One

Your Mindset Can Be A Superpower

Ask any baseball player what goes through their mind when they step up to the plate; if they are thinking about their previous strikeouts, they are much more likely to strike out again. They have to clear their minds of their previous failures in order to focus on the moment to increase their chances of getting a hit.

In the same way, if we keep thinking about all the times when things haven't gone the way we wanted them to and how unhappy we were, then we are in a pattern of negative repetition, and that is more than likely going to be what our future looks like. Instead, we should create a mental picture of what we desire the outcome to be and allow the present and future to unfold as we picture it.

Most people are not comfortable with change. That is unfortunate because change is a fact of life. Strangely, in many cases, people will stay in a job that is not rewarding enough or in a personal relationship they know does not satisfy them. This usually comes from a fear of change and the unknown.

If you have the right mindset, and you remain calm, present, and positive in the NOW, the future will take care of itself. While the future will always remain unknown, it can be treated with a positive feeling of enthusiasm and excitement. Knowing that you are doing the right things for yourself living a healthy lifestyle, eating healthy, and taking the incremental steps that lead to a positive compounding effect helps to create a vision of a bright future.

Have you incorporated positive visualization into your life? Many outcomes come from your predisposition of how a situation will turn out. Think about a high school graduate being accepted to a great university far away from home. For some, the idea of being away from home, family, and friends might be very scary and overwhelming. Imagining being homesick and lonely would probably lead to that sad outcome. Although the student is qualified and is being given a great opportunity, that student might just find themselves at home after one semester. Now imagine another individual with a different mindset. "Wow! Think about all the new friends I'll meet! These students are extremely bright, just like me! Many of them will also be far away from home too. I'll be introduced to new things by them-maybe new music, new food, new ideas!" My guess is that this student is going to have a great experience-not only during those college years. This positive way of thinking allows someone to continue to move forward with new job opportunities and personal relationships as well. Having the right mindset and seeing the future turn out well through positive visualization can help you get what you really want out of life.

> *The greatest discovery of my generation is that human beings can alter their lives by altering their attitudes.*
>
> **WILLIAM JAMES**

> *I discovered that if you expect the worst you will get the worst, and if you expect the best you will get the best.*
>
> **NORMAN VINCENT PEALE**

> *Every strike brings me closer to the next home run.*
>
> **BABE RUTH**

> *You have powers you never dreamed of. You can do things you never thought you could do. There are no limitations in what you can do except the limitations of your own mind.*
>
> **DARWIN P. KINGSLEY**

> *People don't have great attitudes because of great success, they have great success largely because of great attitudes.*
>
> **EARL NIGHTINGALE**

> *Attitude is more important than the past, than education, than money, than circumstances, than what people do or say. It is more important than appearance, giftedness, or skill.*
>
> **W.C. FIELDS**

> *The state of your life is nothing more than a reflection of the state of your mind.*
>
> **WAYNE DYER**

> *I've failed over and over again in my life, and that is why I succeed.*
>
> **MICHAEL JORDAN**

Whether you think you can or you can't, you're right.

HENRY FORD

It is always wise to look ahead, but difficult to look further than you can see.

WINSTON CHURCHILL

> *Everything can be taken from a man but one thing: the last of the human freedoms—to choose one's attitude in any given set of circumstances, to choose one's own way.*
>
> **VIKTOR E. FRANKL**

> *You may not realize it when it happens, but a kick in the teeth may be the best thing in the world for you.*
>
> **WALT DISNEY**

> *I have become my own version of an optimist. If I can't make it through one door, I'll go through another door – or I'll make a door. Something terrific will come no matter how dark the present.*
>
> **RABINDRANATH TAGORE**

> *I measure what's going on, and I adapt to it. I try to get my ego out of the way. The market is smarter than I am so I bend.*
>
> **MARTIN ZWEIG**

Do what you can, with what you have, where you are.

THEODORE ROOSEVELT

Instead of looking at the past, I put myself ahead 20 years and try to look at what I need to do now in order to get there then.

DIANA ROSS

> *The man who rows the boat seldom has time to rock it.*
>
> **BILL COPELAND**

> *Success is going from failure to failure without loss of enthusiasm.*
>
> **WINSTON CHURCHILL**

> *I can't wait until tomorrow 'cause I get better looking every day.*
>
> **JOE NAMATH**

> *I think it is possible for ordinary people to choose to be extraordinary.*
>
> **ELON MUSK**

Chapter Two

Be Your Own Magnet

The Magnet® Stock Selection Process was developed over 25 years ago. My thought was that companies with certain fundamental properties would attract other investors and lead those stocks to higher prices. Several years later, the book *'The Secret'* by Rhonda Byrne came out. I loved the concepts the book introduced and how it applied the same magnetic concepts in a more general way. The book describes the Law of Attraction, which is a powerful reality, but it is critical that we use it the right way.

In this chapter, I'm going to explain how you can start developing an ability to become magnetic and manifest your heart's desires. When I talk about being magnetic, I mean becoming a magnet for your desires to come your way. Attracting what you want from out into the universe. Manifesting those wishes then becomes a second habit for you. That's being magnetic.

I do not believe you can become successful by just imagining you can be. You cannot call an object a magnet unless it has certain metallurgical qualities. In fact, only certain metals can be turned into magnets.

Similarly, if you want to be Magnetic, there are qualities you'll want to develop and possess. If you want to attract the right relationships, have the right opportunities present themselves, and achieve the right outcomes, it requires having the right mindset.

The Law of Attraction suggests that you will attract what you give the most thought to. Strangely, golf pros will tell you if you think about not hitting your ball into the water, guess where the ball tends to go? If, instead, you picture your ball softly landing on the green right next to the pin, your outcome is often a good one. But I'll add that the positive outcome will only happen with a lot of practice. Golf, like life, is not something you should expect to have a good outcome without effort.

An important consideration when thinking magnetically is that you only want to think of and therefore attract what you desire. The way to do that is to control your thoughts and only allow positive thoughts to take hold. You want negative thoughts and negative people to be repelled. You do not even want them to be in any part of your life. It just takes a couple of negative employees to ruin a work environment. Negative teammates can destroy the chemistry of a clubhouse, and companies with negative fundamentals can harm your portfolio.

By keeping a firm hold on what and who you allow into your life, you can improve your personal outcome. I have been investing and managing money for clients for over three decades. Identifying Magnet®

Stocks and managing money is a lot easier than managing the emotions of clients. That is why we take the extra effort to only manage money for clients with a positive mindset. With special regards to all those involved with 'The Secret', Our Magnet® Law of Attraction is to attract only what you want to be attracted to! We can teach ourselves to recognize that, like a Magnet, the law of attraction responds constantly to our thoughts. Be a positive thinker. Be a problem avoider rather than a problem-solver. Think and visualize the positive outcome you desire. Everything happens twice, first in your mind and then in the world around you. Make sure what you put in your mind is what you want to happen. With the right actions and the right behaviors, you will find yourself right where you want to be.

We are similar to magnets in that what you think becomes and attracts you.

JORDAN KIMMEL

The happiest people in life operate out of their imagination and dreams, and not their histories.

ED MYLETT

A man sooner or later discovers that he is the master-gardener of his soul, the director of his life.

JAMES ALLEN

You're at the top when you have made friends with your past, are focused on the present, and are optimistic about your future.

ZIG ZIGLAR

Our acts can be no wiser than our thoughts.

GEORGE CLASON

> *Intellectuals solve problems, geniuses prevent them.*
>
> **ALBERT EINSTEIN**

> *Don't let anyone determine your fate.*
>
> **BILL MCDERMOTT**

> *Whatever you believe about yourself on the inside, is what will manifest on the outside.*
>
> **JOHN ASSARAF**

> *You cannot control the outcome. You can only control the effort and the dedication and the giving of one hundred percent of yourself to the task at hand. And then whatever happens, happens.*
>
> **TOM GAYNOR**

> *Your mind can be either your prison or your palace. What you make it is yours to decide.*
>
> **BERNARD KELVIN CLIVE**

> *The mind is everything. What you think you become.*
>
> **BUDDHA**

> *Decide what you want. Believe you can have it. Believe you deserve it and believe it's possible for you.*
>
> **JACK CANFIELD**

> *Everything comes to him who hustles while he waits.*
>
> **THOMAS EDISON**

> *It is a funny thing about life; if you refuse to accept anything but the best, you very often get it.*
>
> **W. SOMERSET MAUGHAM**

> *To achieve goals you've never achieved before, you need to start doing things you've never done before.*
>
> **STEPHEN COVEY**

> *Creativity is intelligence having fun.*
>
> **ALBERT EINSTEIN**

> *No person was ever honored for what he received. Honor has been the reward for what he gave.*
>
> **CALVIN COOLIDGE**

> *Any investment manager who tells you they know what will happen in the future is kidding you and themselves. Know what is going on NOW!*
>
> **JORDAN KIMMEL**

> *Invest in yourself! That is the best investment you can make.*
>
> **SETH KIMMEL**

Chapter Three

Living A Happy Life

It seems to be human conditioning to believe that when I get enough money, or the right partner, or fill in the blank with whatever it is, I'll be happy. If we aren't happy NOW chances are we won't be happy then. These conditions make us reliant on something outside ourselves that we think will make us happy.

It's debatable whether money can buy happiness. Some people swear by the old platitude that it can't, whereas others are adamant that money can be used to buy happiness. However, that's not what I want to discuss in this chapter.

For me, the essence of being happy is more about being able to enjoy "where I am" and "who I am". I see too many people trying to compare themselves to others. In this world of social media comparisons, and a focus on materialistic possessions can drive feelings of insecurity and lead to depression.

One of my sons likes to say "happiness is over-rated". He likes to say to become truly successful and achieve what you desire you need to be willing to be uncomfortable.

Certain periods of life can be challenging and while you are sweating things out, times are not always easy. I try not to confuse being challenged with being unhappy. In fact, being aware that excellent outcomes often follow great challenges, my internal mindset is to enjoy the process. I think that if you can keep a positive attitude, smile through adversity, get up when you are knocked down, and keep your eye on the prize, very little can keep you from being happy NOW!

Attending The Bronx High School of Science was a real eye opener for me. The school has a notoriously difficult entrance exam and only accepts the top students in New York City. If you passed the test, admission was free. You can only imagine how desirable the school was and every year thousands of students took the test. While my family was thrilled when I was admitted, the school taught me more than just strong academics. What I found out soon enough was that most of the students were way smarter than me, or way-way smarter than me! But I also noticed many of them were somewhat socially awkward and I would not trade places with them in life, regardless of how much higher their test scores were. Then there were still others who were not only smarter than me but also "better looking", a foot taller than me, and far better at chess than I was. I learned then that there is always "a faster gun in town" and that being comfortable in my own skin is the key to my happiness. I was still pretty cool and I knew it!

Beware of destination addiction, a preoccupation with the idea that happiness is in the next place, the next job, and with the next partner. Until you give up the idea that happiness is somewhere else, it will never be where you are.

ROBERT HOLDEN

A happy man is too satisfied with the present to dwell too much on the future.

ALBERT EINSTEIN

Happiness shouldn't be a goal, it should be a habit.

RICHARD BRANSON

Eat well, move more, stress less, love more.

DR. DEAN ORNISH

Happiness is like a butterfly which, when pursued, is always beyond our grasp, but, if you will sit down quietly, may alight upon you.

NATHANIEL HAWTHORNE

The great science to live happily is to live in the present.

PYTHAGORAS

> *Happiness is not something you postpone for the future; it is something you design for the present.*
>
> **JIM ROHN**

> *There is no way to happiness, happiness is the way.*
>
> **WAYNE DYER**

A smile is the best makeup a girl could wear.

MARILYN MONROE

Be happy with what you have. Be excited about what you want.

ALAN COHEN

Happiness depends upon ourselves.

ARISTOTLE

All the happiness and fulfilment that humans yearn for exists in the present moment.

DEEPAK CHOPRA

Happiness is a habit—cultivate it.

ELBERT HUBBARD

Success is getting what you want. Happiness is wanting what you get.

DALE CARNEGIE

> *Be happy in the moment, that's enough. Each moment is all we need, not more.*
>
> **MOTHER TERESA**

> *Happiness, not in another place but this place... not for another hour, but this hour.*
>
> **WALT WHITMAN**

Chapter Four

Present Moment Living

Be proactive and make it your mission to concentrate on the here and NOW at all times. Being proactive is a skill that leads to great success. Therefore, in many situations, you won't need to search for the NOW since you'll already be in it.

You leave the house in the NOW, and you make a conscious decision to keep yourself in the NOW throughout the day. If you need a physical reminder, try putting a rubber band around your wrist and snapping it every so often.

You could make it a routine to snap the rubber band and use it as a signal to bring your attention back to the NOW. Or any other reminder that will bring your attention to the events that are transpiring at this very NOW.

The Magical Power of Compounding

Pick one - $1,000,000 today or 1 penny doubled for 30 days. Which one would you pick? Now, if you have heard this penny example before, you know the answer should be the penny doubled for 30 days.

The reward of compounding is getting huge rewards from making a lot of small smart choices. We can use it to improve our finances, health, relationships, and just about anything else. The changes can seem so small that you might not even notice them. That's why these small incremental steps can be so easy to take! While there is usually no big instant win that comes right away, the long-term benefits can be surprising.

Over time, just like compound interest, taking personal and positive small steps can create a radical difference. The results of compounding take time, and that's OK! A mistake is that often people give up quickly on making positive personal changes because they don't see results overnight. Maybe that is where the expression "patience is a virtue" comes in.

The tough thing about letting your money grow through compounding is that some people give up when they don't see results happening fast enough. They make a mistake by being focused on instant gratification. For those who can keep making progress, understanding "Rome wasn't built in a day", a few years later, the results are almost impossible to imagine. The same results will happen when you are aware of the present moment, "NOW", and keep going.

NOW, go and start compounding your NOWs!

The best time to plant a tree was 20 years ago. The second best time is now.

CHINESE PROVERB

We can make excellent investment decisions on the basis of present observations, with no need to make guesses about the future.

HOWARD MARKS

Eighty percent of success is showing up.

WOODY ALLEN

Put the past behind you, the present moment is all that matters, in the life of those who want to be happy.

LEON BROWN

> *Life is what happens while you are busy making other plans.*
>
> **JOHN LENNON**

> *It makes no difference how many peaks you reach if there was no pleasure in the climb.*
>
> **OPRAH WINFREY**

Ask yourself what "problem" you have right now, not next year, tomorrow, or five minutes from now. What is wrong with this moment?

ECKHART TOLLE

Life is a one-way journey to be enjoyed, so enjoy the beauty of the present moment with all your heart.

DEBASISH MRIDHA

> *What we need is a selection of sensible habits that give us a marginal advantage that will compound over time.*
>
> **WILLIAM GREEN**

> *Forget about perfection; focus on progression, and compound the improvements.*
>
> **DAVID BRAILSFORD**

My father was the richest person I've ever known, and it's not because he had more money than Jeff Bezos or Warren Buffett. But he had enough. That's a psychological statement.

TOM GAYNOR

This is a wonderful day. I have never seen this one before.

MAYA ANGELOU

> *To live in the present moment is a miracle. The miracle is not to walk on water. The miracle is to walk on the green Earth in the present moment, to appreciate the peace and beauty that are available now.*
>
> **THICH NHAT HANH**

> *The mystery of human existence lies not in just staying alive, but in finding something to live for.*
>
> **FYODOR DOSTOYEVSKY**

Forever is composed of Nows.

EMILY DICKINSON

Few of us ever live in the present. We are forever anticipating what is to come or remembering what has gone.

LOUIS L'AMOUR

Chapter Five

Meditation

Press Reset, and tap into your power. Meditation has a major impact on our subconscious mind, which is the seat of boundless creativity and limitless riches in our lives. Through the practice of meditation, our subconscious mind may be reprogrammed, paving the way for more success and pleasure in our lives.

The part of our mind known as the subconscious is the layer of our mind that the contents are not easily accessible; yet, the conscious mind is often reminded of aspects of the subconscious. These include our recollections, our abilities, our routines, and any other internal inclinations we may have.

The unconscious part of our minds is where all of our untapped potential and creative energy is stored. The mental chatter that is always going on in our conscious mind is the source of the issue, since it prevents us from accessing this latent potential. Things will only emerge from the great depths of the subconscious when the conscious mind is free of clutter and distractions.

A simple form of meditation is to focus on your breathing. Have you ever wondered why every meditation you listen to encourages you to take deep breaths? Sure, it's relaxing. But is there more to it? Breathing is so fundamental to our lives that we frequently forget that there is no life without it. When we control our breath, it tells our psyche that there's nothing that we cannot control. There's no uncertainty. There's nothing we really need to be concerned about. A simple act of taking some deep breaths can become one of the most healing and empowering experiences of your life if you do it with awareness of the power of your breath.

When you pause your breath, you pause your life. Try the breathing pattern of 4-4-4. Here's how it works:

- Inhale deeply for four seconds.

- Hold your breath for four seconds.

- Exhale slowly for four seconds.... Repeat

Continue to breathe, and return your attention back to your breathing and the awareness you've created. Whenever you notice that your attention is drifting away, just go back to noticing your inhalations and exhalations. If you make this a daily practice, you will train your mind to focus on whatever you need it to focus on. We are able to choose the life we desire to live when we are focused.

> *Even in the middle of a hurricane, the bottom of the sea is calm. As the storm rages and the winds howl, the deep waters sway in gentle rhythm, a light movement of fish and plant life. Below there is no storm.*
>
> **WAYNE MULLER**

> *Meditation is the single greatest technology I know of for investors seeking alpha. It is more important than the proper investment philosophy, proper techniques, or even years of experience.*
>
> **JASON VOSS**

Practices for sustained high performance have a compounding effect. The reason you meditate is not because it's important on a given day. The regular practice of meditation will help you handle the hard setbacks and will keep you constantly prepared for them…Having that practice in place prepares you well. It's a lot like preventive medicine.

SHUBIN STEIN

The cyclone derives its power from a calm center. So does a person.

NORMAN VINCENT PEALE

The more tranquil a man becomes, the greater is his success, his influence, his power for good. Calmness of mind is one of the beautiful jewels of wisdom.

JAMES ALLEN

Yoga introduced me to a style of meditation. The only meditation I would have done before would be in the writing of songs.

STING

> *After being a father, son, spouse and business owner serving others for decades I've learned the best way to avoid the "keep everyone happy" trap is to meditate on a regular basis with the intention of separating what my ego wants to control from what is meant to unfold creatively.*
>
> **COLBY MCFADDEN**

> *Most persons are so absorbed in the contemplation of the outside world that they're wholly oblivious to what's passing on within themselves.*
>
> **NIKOLA TESLA**

When you're a kid, you lay in the grass and watch the clouds going over, and you literally don't have a thought in your mind. It's purely meditation, and we lose that.

DICK VAN DYKE

Now and then it's good to pause in our pursuit of happiness and just be happy.

GUILLAUME APOLLINAIRE

The goal of meditation isn't to control your thoughts, it's to stop letting them control you.

ANONYMOUS

To live happily is an inward power of the soul.

MARCUS AURELIUS

The successful warrior is the average man, with laser-like focus.

BRUCE LEE

Your beliefs become your thoughts, your thoughts become your words, your words become your actions, your actions become your habits, your habits become your values, your values become your destiny.

MAHATMA GANDHI

Feelings come and go like clouds in a windy sky. Conscious breathing is my anchor.

THICH NHAT HANH

Everyone wants to live on top of the mountain, but all the happiness and growth occurs while you're climbing it.

ANDY ROONEY

Chapter Six

Being Mindful in your Personal and Professional Life by Ritika Hiranandani

Being 'MINDFUL' is the practice of focusing your attention on the present moment. Your mind can be your best friend or your worst enemy.

Mindfulness is now being examined scientifically and has been found to reduce stress and enhance overall happiness.

Practicing mindfulness can be done through meditation, prayer, introspection, and being aware of the present moment.

You have absolute control over just one thing, your mind. This divine gift is the sole means by which you may conquer your destiny.

The more mindful a person becomes, the greater is his success, his influence, and his power for good. Conquering the mind is one of the beautiful jewels of wisdom.

Leaders who provide mindfulness resources for their team members often experience increased productivity.

Focus on reaching out to the inner core of your existence:

- What is your purpose?
- Why are you here?
- What have you learned from your past?
- How do you imagine your future?
- Do you absorb, process, reflect, express, and share what you learn?

Learning from your past, focusing on your goals, and engaging in your present 'NOW' requires meditative practices, a conscious effort, and an ongoing habit of being mindful.

I aspire to live in the energy of the present moment, bringing in the mindfulness of the 'NOW'.

Live in the moment. Try to intentionally bring an open, accepting, and discerning attention to everything you do.

About Ritika Hiranandani

Ritika is a business strategist certified by the Harvard Business School. She is passionate about identifying opportunities, creating revenue generating action plans, and implementing funding strategies that are aligned with core business objectives. She advises clients to build mindful strategic solutions based on data insights to achieve pragmatic goals.

She has more than 20 years of experience in formulating business relationships, resulting in structured, result-oriented strategic plans for several projects in the fields of e-commerce, finance, healthcare, and e-sports.

> *By being more mindful in your everyday life, you achieve a higher purpose and greater contentment.*
>
> **RITIKA HIRANANDANI**

> *We cannot solve our problems with the same thinking we used when we created them.*
>
> **ALBERT EINSTEIN**

> *I've learned... That love, not time, heals all wounds.*
>
> **ANDY ROONEY**

> *I have realized that the past and future are real illusions, that they exist in the present, which is what there is and all there is.*
>
> **ALAN WATTS**

> *Every moment is a fresh beginning.*
>
> **T.S. ELIOT**

Be willing to be a beginner every single morning.

MEISTER ECKHART

Each moment is a place you've never been.

MARK STRAND

> *The present is the point at which time touches eternity.*
>
> **C.S. LEWIS**

> *Your time is limited, so don't waste it living someone else's life.*
>
> **STEVE JOBS**

> *To meditate with mindful breathing is to bring body and mind back to the present moment so that you do not miss your appointment with life.*
>
> **THICH NHAT HANH**

> *You have absolute control over just one thing, your thoughts. This divine gift is the sole means by which you may control your destiny. If you fail to control your mind, you will control nothing else.*
>
> **NAPOLEON HILL**

> *You can dramatically extend life—not by multiplying the number of your years, but by expanding the fullness of your moments.*
>
> **SHINZEN YOUNG**

> *Be silent or let thy words be worth more than silence.*
>
> **PYTHAGORAS**

INVEST IN THE NOW

Chapter Seven

Start Investing NOW
Five Questions and Answers to Help Get Started

I have worked in the financial industry for more than 30 years, helping other people invest. During those years, and long before I even entered the business, I tried to read and learn from the best investors that came before me.

While there are various styles of investing and different lessons to be learned, I found that I heard many of the same questions from people just starting to invest. Here, I answer the five questions I've been asked the most. These are the thoughts I shared with my own children. I hope that they are helpful to them, as well as you.

While I share my personal answers to these questions, we also asked Sam Stovall, one of the most respective investors of this era. These may not be the questions or answers that resonate with you personally. That's OK. Our intent is to help everyone begin their journey of achieving financial security, which can help you to live happily in the NOW.

Investing sounds like something my parents or grandparents did. I do not make enough money to invest now. When should I really get started?

Answer: You do not need a lot of money to get started. Like lots of things in life, there are lessons to be learned, and the earlier you get started the sooner you learn from beginner mistakes. Just like playing chess or gardening, nothing beats hands-on experience. Lessons learned early will give you the knowledge and confidence to operate confidently when you have more capital behind you in the future. Just as importantly, it amazes people when they see evidence of the effects of compounded returns over time. Slowly accumulating assets early has a profound impact on the ability of wealth generation over time.

Investing seems so complicated and confusing. How can I really get started?

Answer: Like many other subjects, reading and learning from the most successful individuals in any given field is a great place to start. There are many lessons to be learned from many investors who created great wealth for themselves and who have been willing to share their methods and mindset to guide the next generations. Most of them have started with modest means and feel an obligation to help others. Jim Rogers is one example. Try to read every book he wrote—it's a good place to start!

In my first book, *Magnet Investing*, written over 20 years ago, I included a list of over 50 recommended books that I think every potential investor should read. Since then, I have read well over another 100 books and continue to enjoy the insights of other successful investors to this day. Technology has taken care of that for those who say they simply have no time to read. Audiobooks and podcasts can be your alternative. Like our own Magnet Minutes Podcast. Visit: *www.valuenginecapital-jordankimmel.com/podcast-1*

Isn't the stock market just one big casino? I don't have money to gamble away…

Answer: The stock market is not a gambling casino. The odds are not stacked against you like they are in a casino. There is no "house" that takes a cut on each hand you play. Instead, the stock market operates as a clearing house that allows investors to buy and sell pieces of companies and to passively own companies that can generate passive income and wealth for you over time. While some people trade stocks actively, other investors look for the profitable companies in a wide variety of industries and let the experienced management of those companies help them earn wealth as a "part owner of the company".

Isn't investing really time-consuming? I am too busy to watch the markets…

Answer: Investing does not need to be overly time consuming at all. While it is always a good idea to keep current on the overall conditions of the world and economy, by simply monitoring your personal investments for a couple of hours every few months, you will be fine.

If I want to invest in the stock market, what is a good way to get started?

Answer: My suggestion is to treat the stock market as a wealth accumulation vehicle. I would avoid investing in too many individual stocks at the outset. Instead, I would identify a few mutual funds or ETFs that represent different aspects of the economy—technology, healthcare, and communications are good examples. You can dollar cost average into these funds by investing a small amount every few months. Dollar-cost averaging is a great way to take the emotion out of investing and gives you the discipline to keep accumulating wealth slowly.

If you can find a couple of companies that you believe are dominant in their industry, you can also make a small investment in those shares as well. Try to avoid anything that seems like a fad, even if it seems "hot at the moment". While you will want to monitor these companies to make sure year-over-year revenue growth continues, just a couple of well-placed investments in the best companies can create wealth over 10-20 years that is hard to even anticipate!

It could also be a good idea to invest in your local electric utility company. These companies do not present fast tickets to wealth but are instead heavily regulated companies. They are regulated to be profitable! Utilities pay dividends, and those dividends will increase over time. Years later, when your investment in your local utility has grown along with your dividend payments, your monthly bill won't bother you too much either!

The 5 questions answered by Sam Stovall, Chief Investment Officer of CFRA

Investing sounds like something my parents or grandparents did. I do not make enough money to invest now, when should I really get started?

Answer: The best time to start investing was 10 years ago. The second-best time is today. That's all because of the power of compounding.

Investing seems so complicated and confusing. How can I really get started?

Answer: Buy (and read) the book before you buy (or sell) the stock. The only way to get a "cut of the action" is by being an owner. Learning the basics behind investing can be both fun and rewarding.

Isn't the stock market just one big casino? I don't have money to gamble away…

Answer: The S&P 500 has recorded positive annual total returns (price plus dividends) about 80% of the time since WWII. If investing is gambling, I'd love to learn which casino pays the gambler 80% of the time!

Isn't investing really time-consuming? I am too busy to watch the markets…

Answer: Investing is a journey. Either you can do the driving (where you select and control the investment vehicles) or you let someone else do it (through a mutual fund or a professionally managed portfolio).

If I want to invest in the stock market, what is a good way to get started?

Answer: Invest in what you know. Do you have a keen eye for fashion? Focus on retailing stocks. Do you focus on food? Sink your teeth into restaurant stocks. Leverage your strengths!

> *Saving for retirement is simply deferring consumption – putting away the cost of living today to enjoy in later years. However, the only proven way to outpace inflation and taxes is through investing in equities.*
>
> **SAM STOVALL**

It wasn't raining when Noah built the ark.

WARREN BUFFETT

Those who can not adjust to change will be swept aside by it. Those who recognize change and react accordingly will benefit.

JIM ROGERS

To be a successful investor you really need to understand psychology and history. Very often emotions drive the market up or down. Remember that economies and markets are two very different things.

JIM ROGERS

When we concern ourselves not only with our own self-interest but with that of all of the stakeholders involved, including society and our planet, we have more powerful returns and not only monetarily.

KIM ANN CURTIN

An investment in knowledge pays the best interest.

BENAMIN FRANKLIN

Significance of the Number 108

So what's the deal with the number 108? You'd be surprised that a seemingly innocuous number carries so much meaning.

One represents a new path towards progress, becoming a leader, and taking initiative. Zero by itself is said to represent nothingness, but if you put it alongside other numbers, it boosts the vibrations of those numbers. Eight relates to power–the power of manifestation, and the ability to become influential in certain areas of our lives. Eight also represents infinity–if you flip it sideways, you get the infinity symbol.

But there's more.

Mathematician Leonardo Fibonacci theorized that the number 108 represents the wholeness of existence. It's also known as the "universal rule of nature" and "nature's secret code", governing dimensions like the Great Pyramid of Giza.

108 has a lot of significance in both religious and spiritual institutions. For example, Buddhist priests

must ring a bell 108 times at the end of the year. This represents the 108 temptations you need to resist to reach enlightenment. Hindu deities have 108 names they're referred to, and mantras are said 108 times by Hindus.

In astrology, the number 108 is also significant. There are 12 houses for each of the zodiac signs, along with the nine planets that navigate those houses. Can you guess what 12 times nine is?

Yes! 108!

The Silver metal acts as a representative of the moon. Guess what the atomic weight of Silver is?

That's right! 108.

Or think about the number of days in a leap year. When you multiply each individual number (three times six times six), you get 108.

Get this: both the Sun and the moon's diameter can be multiplied by 108 to measure the distance between them and the Earth.

The number 108 is also important in the physical realm. For instance, your body will shut down if the internal temperature is at 108°F. Why? You run the risk of developing brain damage, which will cause convulsions and ultimately lead to death.

Now for the sports lovers out there: There are 108 stitches on a baseball. This allows one side of the baseball to gain a higher velocity. The ball's movement doesn't sway from its trajectory, and it prepares the ball for a curve by spinning. For this reason, American professional baseball clubs only use balls that have this pattern with 108 stitches.

The reason why 108 carries such significance is because so much of life revolves around it. From the way our bodies function to how the planets are constructed, 108 is a pretty impactful number. Without it, life would look totally different. The planets would be organized in a different way, our bodies would regulate themselves in a potentially harmful manner, and we wouldn't be able to fully immerse ourselves in the now.

Take the 108 temptations of Buddhism. Would you be able to identify them if it wasn't for the number 108? Or would some other seemingly arbitrary number be assigned to them to advise followers to avoid these temptations as they seek enlightenment?

The next time you see the number 108, think of how so many things in nature are held together because of that number.

The number 108 is clearly embedded deeply in human consciousness.

Epilogue

Summing it all up and sharing it

In 1987, during my second job on Wall Street, I had a stunning view from my office window. It overlooked the statue of George Washington facing The New York Stock Exchange on the corners of Wall Street and Broad Street. Although my interest was in the stock market, my firm was primarily involved with selling municipal bonds to clients around the country. The sales manager would remind us to share with clients that the firm was not only in New York, but on Wall Street, which is only six blocks long. There was something super cool about the address and the view!

In my book *The Magnet Method of Investing*, I shared meeting with Seth Glickenhaus. He was in his mid-90's and had been managing a mutual fund for over 45 years! Obviously, he was already extremely successful and wealthy. Glickenhaus continued to love the profession, as the great challenge of the markets never leaves certain people. Similarly, I met with Michael Steinhardt even though he shared he was retired at the time. I was surprised to see a small army of traders working at his office, but maybe I should not have been. If you have spent most of your life studying and trading the market, it is uncommon to lose interest. I feel the same way.

EPILOGUE

Over the last 35 years, I have personally met with many of the top investors of this generation and read hundreds of investment books. I have also been an avid reader of many other subjects. This book is an attempt to give back and share the knowledge and experience gained over these decades. Much of the knowledge and most of the quotes come from others. As they say, I am simply standing on the backs of greats.

On a recent walk, I came across a new fountain that was placed on the extreme East side of Wall Street as a memorial to the tragedy of 9/11. For me, the fountain represents the feeling of "my cup runneth" over. I think about all the great traders and investors that walked the narrow caverns of Wall Street. Not all have been as lucky in life as I have been. I have learned to take nothing for granted and how grateful I am to be in the place I am.

As we go to print with this book, there are all kinds of dark clouds and disturbances in the air. The stock market is in a bear cycle, there is war in Europe, and the world is trying to emerge from a global pandemic and a virus that has caused tremendous mental health issues. This is a tough time for many. Most young people are afraid to invest, especially now. This book and the quotes will hopefully instill some confidence and guidance. Not only are we trying to provide some investment wisdom, but we are also thinking about others overall well-being. From the team at Magnet, who are grateful that our cup is full, we hope these quotes and guidance can be of help to you- and may your cup runneth over as well!

REFERENCE LEGEND

Woody Allen (American comedian and playwright) – page 48

James Allen (British philosophical writer known for his inspirational books and poetry and as a pioneer of the self-help movement) – page 26, 59

Maya Angelou (American memoirist, popular poet, and civil rights activist) – page 52

Guillaume Apollinaire (French poet, playwright, short story writer, novelist, and art critic of Polish-Belarusian descent) – page 61

Aristotle (Greek philosopher and polymath. Taught by Plato) – page 42

John Assaraf (American motivational speaker and trainer) – page 29

Marcus Aurelius (Roman Emperor) – page 62

David Brailsford (British cycling and performance coach) – page 51

Richard Branson (British billionaire, entrepreneur, and business magnate) – page 38

Leon Brown (Author of All Are Welcome) – page 48

Buddha (Spiritual teacher of ancient India) – page 30

Warren Buffett (CEO of Berkshire Hathaway) – page 81

Jack Canfield (American author, motivational speaker, corporate trainer, and entrepreneur) – page 31

Dale Carnegie (American lecturer and author of How to Win Friends and Influence People) – page 43

Deepak Chopra (Indian-American author and alternative medicine advocate) – page 42

Winston Churchill (British statesman, soldier and Prime Minister of the United Kingdom) – page 17, 21

George Clason (Author of The Richest Man in Babylon) – page 27

Bernard Kelvin Clive (Author, Speaker, Trainer , and Lecturer from Ghana) – page 30

Alan Cohen (American poet who founded and edited the San Francisco Oracle) – page 41

Calvin Coolidge (30th president of the United States, from 1923 to 1929) – page 33

Bill Copeland (American poet, writer, and historian) – page 21

Stephen Covey (American educator, author, businessman, and keynote speaker) – page 32

Kim Ann Curtin (Founder of The Wall Street Coach and author of Transforming Wall Street) – page 82

Emily Dickinson (American poet) – page 54

Walt Disney (American film producer and entrepreneur, founder of The Disney Company) – page 18

Fyodor Dostoyevsky (Russian novelist, short story writer, essayist, and journalist) – page 53

Wayne Dyer (American self-help author and a motivational speaker) – page 16, 40

Meister Eckart (German Catholic theologian, philosopher, and mystic) – page 70

Thomas Edison (American inventor and businessman) – page 31

Albert Einstein (German-born physicist, most influential physicist of all time) – page 28, 33, 37, 68

T.S. Eliot (Poet, essayist, publisher, playwright, literary critic) – page 69

W.C. Fields (American comedian and actor) – page 15

Henry Ford (American industrialist and founder of The Ford Motor Company) – page 17

Viktor E. Frankl (Founder of logotherapy) – page 18

Benjamin Franklin (Iconic American polymath who was active as a writer, scientist, inventor, statesman, diplomat, printer, publisher, and political philosopher. A Founding Father of America) – page 82

Mahatma Gandhi (Indian lawyer, anti-colonial nationalist, and political ethicist) – page 63

Tom Gaynor (Co-Chief Executive Officer of Markel Corporation) – page 29, 52

William Green (Author of Richer, Wiser, Happier) – page 51

Thich Nhat Hanh (Vietnamese Thiền Buddhist monk, peace activist, author, poet) – page 53, 64, 72

Nathaniel Hawthorne (American novelist and short story writer) – page 39

Napoleon Hill (American self-help author best known for his book Think and Grow Rich) – page 72

Ritika Hiranandani (Entrepreneur/business strategist certified by the Harvard Business School) page 67

Robert Holden (British psychologist, author, and broadcaster) – page 37

Elbert Hubbard (American writer, publisher, artist, and philosopher) – page 43

William James (American philosopher, historian, and psychologist) – page 13

Steve Jobs (Co-founder, chairman, and CEO of Apple) – page 71

Michael Jordan (American businessman and former professional basketball legend) – page 16

Jordan Kimmel (Market Strategist and portfolio manager at ValuEngine Capital) – page 5, 25, 34

Seth Kimmel (Software engineer) – page 34

Darwin P. Kingsley (American insurance executive) – page 14

Louis L'Amour (American novelist and short story writer) – page 54

Bruce Lee (Hong Kong and American martial artist/instructor, actor, and philosopher) – page 63

John Lennon (English singer, songwriter, and musician who achieved fame with The Beatles) – page 49

C.S. Lewis (British writer and Anglican lay theologian) – page 71

Howard Marks (Chairman and co-founder of Oaktree) – page 47

W. Somerset Maugham (English writer, known for his plays, novels, and short stories) – page 32

Bill McDermott (American businessman, currently CEO of ServiceNow) – page 28

Colby McFadden (Founder of Quiver Financial) – page 60

Marilyn Monroe (American actress and national icon) – page 41

Mother Teresa (Saint Teresa of Calcutta, was an Albanian-Indian Roman Catholic nun) – page 44

Debasish Mridha (Accomplished entrepreneur, philanthropist, and author) – page 50

Wayne Muller (An executive leadership mentor, therapist, minister, and bestselling author) – page 57

Elon Musk (Business magnate, visionary, and investor) – page 22

Ed Mylett (Global Entrepeneur and bestselling Author) – page 26

Joe Namath (Quarterback New York Jets, MVP of Super Bowl III) – page 22

Earl Nightingale (American radio speaker and author) – page 15

Dr. Dean Ornish (American physician and researcher) – page 38

Norman Vincent Peale (Author best known for popularizing the concept of positive thinking, author of The Power of Positive Thinking) – page 13, 58

Pythagoras (Greek philosopher) – page 39

Jim Rogers (American investor and financial commentator, author of "must read books") – page 81

Jim Rohn (American author, salesman, and motivational speaker) – page 40

Andy Rooney (American radio and television writer, 60 Minutes icon) – page 64, 68

Theodore Roosevelt (26th US President, from 1901 to 1909) – page 20

Diana Ross (American singer and actress) – page 20

Babe Ruth (Legendary American baseball player) – page 14

Shubin Stein (Founder and chairman of Spencer Capital Management) – page 58

Sting (British musician who found fame with the band The Police) – page 59

Sam Stovall (Chief Investment Strategist of CFRA) – page 80

Mark Strand (Canadian-born American essayist and poet) – page 70

Rabindranath Tagore (Known for remodeling Indian art with modernism in the 20th century) – page 19

Nikola Tesla (Serbian-American inventor, electrical and mechanical engineer, and futurist) – page 60

Eckhart Tolle (German-born spiritual teacher) – page 50

Mark Twain (Pen name for Samuel Clemens; American writer, humorist, entrepreneur) – page 2

Dick Van Dyke (American actor, singer, dancer, and comedian) – page 61

Jason Voss (CEO, Deception and Truth Analysis) – page 57

Alan Watts (American poet, essayist, and journalist) – page 69

Walt Whitman (American poet, essayist, and journalist) – page 44

Oprah Winfrey (American talk show host, television producer, author, and philanthropist) – page 49

Shinzen Young (American meditation teacher) – page 73

Zig Ziglar (American author, salesman, and motivational speaker) – page 27

Martin Zweig (American stock investor, investment adviser, and financial analyst) – page 19

For those interested in help with investing

Jordan is the Chief Equity Strategist and Portfolio Manager at ValuEngine Capital Management. ValuEngine Capital Management is a Registered Investment Advisory headquartered in Melbourne, Florida.

Please e-mail Jordan directly at to set up a personal consultation or start a conversation.

jkimmel@valuenginecapital.com

You can read other articles describing the Magnet® Stock Selection Process and see many of Jordan's television appearances at:

www.valuenginecapital-jordankimmel.com

You can follow Jordan's commentary by subscribing to Magnet Minutes Podcast:

www.valuenginecapital-jordankimmel.com/podcast-1

Jordan's two previous books have been widely endorsed in the financial community and can provide an excellent foundation for investors:

The MAGNET Method of Investing
Find, Trade, and Profit from Exceptional Stocks

Magnet Investing
Build a Portfolio and Pick Winning Stocks Using Your Home Computer

www.ingramcontent.com/pod-product-compliance
Lightning Source LLC
Chambersburg PA
CBHW050241220526
45465CB00002B/510